INSECTS: SIX-LEGGED NIGHTMARES

JEWEL WASPS TAKE OVER!

BY CAITIE MCANENEY

Gareth Stevens
PUBLISHING

Please visit our website, www.garethstevens.com. For a free color catalog of all our high-quality books, call toll free 1-800-542-2595 or fax 1-877-542-2596.

Cataloging-in-Publication Data

Names: McAneney, Caitie.
Title: Jewel wasps take over! / Caitie McAneney.
Description: New York : Gareth Stevens Publishing, 2018. | Series: Insects: six-legged nightmares | Includes index.
Identifiers: ISBN 9781538212677 (pbk.) | ISBN 9781538212691 (library bound) | ISBN 9781538212684 (6 pack)
Subjects: LCSH: Wasps–Juvenile literature.
Classification: LCC QL565.2 M286 2018 | DDC 595.79'8–dc23

First Edition

Published in 2018 by
Gareth Stevens Publishing
111 East 14th Street, Suite 349
New York, NY 10003

Copyright © 2018 Gareth Stevens Publishing

Designer: Laura Bowen
Editor: Ryan Nagelhout/Kate Mikoley

Photo credits: Cover, p. 1 (jewel wasp) Frank Greenaway/Dorling Kindersley/Getty Images; cover, p. 1 (background leaves) Wasant/Shutterstock.com; cover, pp. 1–24 (background) Fantom666/Shutterstock.com; cover, pp. 1–24 (black splatter) Miloje/Shutterstock.com; pp. 4–24 (text boxes) Tueris/Shutterstock.com; p. 5 (main) Muhammad Mahdi Karim/Wikimedia Commons; p. 5 (inset) fotorawin/Shutterstock.com; pp. 7, 11, 15 Anand Varma/National Geographic/Getty Images; p. 9 sirabhop/Shutterstock.com; p. 13 Glass and Nature/Shutterstock.com; p. 17 (top) ananaline/Shutterstock.com; p. 17 (bottom) NeagoneFo/Shutterstock.com; p. 19 Barnaby Chambers/Shutterstock.com; p. 21 nounours/Shutterstock.com.

Printed in China

CPSIA compliance information: Batch #CW18GS. For further information contact Gareth Stevens, New York, New York at 1-800-542-2595.

CONTENTS

Every Cockroach's Nightmare. 4

Tiny Wasp 6

Finding a Jewel Wasp 8

Let the Hunt Begin 10

Brain Surgery 12

Planting Eggs 14

An Inside Job 16

Jewel Wasps and People. 18

A Deadly Sting 20

Glossary. 22

For More Information 23

Index 24

Words in the glossary appear in **bold** type the first time they are used in the text.

EVERY COCKROACH'S NIGHTMARE

There's no match for the jewel wasp. This **insect** is a skilled killer. It enslaves its **victim**, usually a cockroach, and plants a baby wasp in its body. The tiny, brightly colored wasp leads the cockroach to its death. This insect might be tiny, but it's certainly a nightmare.

Jewel wasps are parasites, or creatures that live off other animals, often causing harm or death. Over millions of years, parasites have **developed** ways to get what they want from their **host**.

TERRIFYING TRUTHS

The jewel wasp is also called the emerald cockroach wasp.

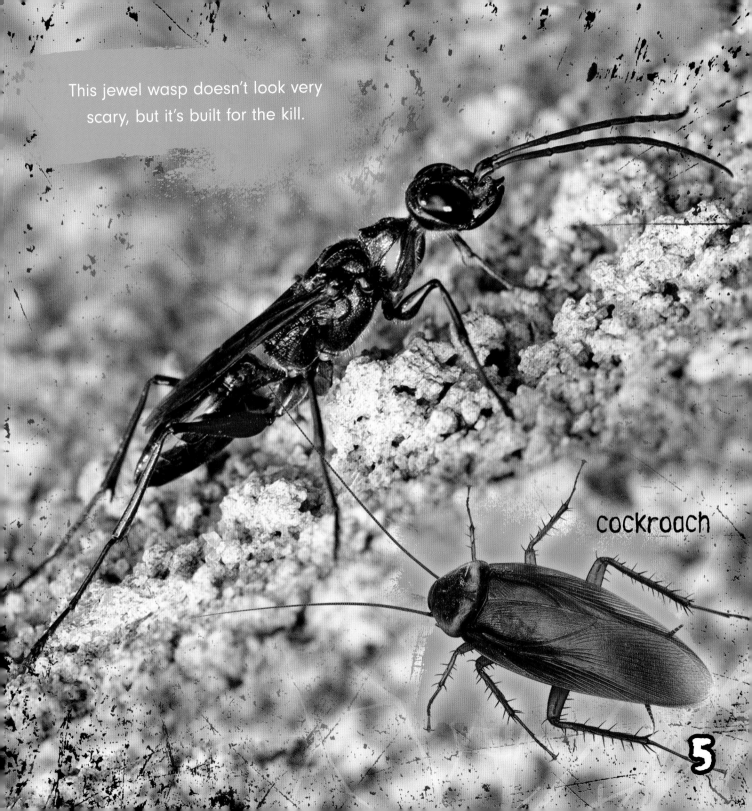

This jewel wasp doesn't look very scary, but it's built for the kill.

cockroach

5

TINY WASP

Jewel wasps are mostly blue green with red on certain parts of their body. Like all insects, they have six legs and three main body parts: the head, a middle part called the thorax, and a rear part called the abdomen. They also have small wings, antennae, and a stinger.

Jewel wasps grow to be less than 1 inch (2.5 cm) long. Even so, they're able to kill flies and cockroaches that are much larger. They show that smaller insects can still cause harm.

TERRIFYING TRUTHS

Female jewel wasps are bigger than males.
Male jewel wasps don't have a stinger.

6

PARTS OF A JEWEL WASP

head

legs

abdomen

antenna

eye

thorax

wings

stinger

The tops of the jewel wasp's legs are red.

FINDING A JEWEL WASP

The jewel wasp is native to parts of Africa and Asia. Luckily for American cockroaches, these insects aren't found in most of North or South America.

You can also find jewel wasps in Hawaii and the Cook Islands in the Pacific Ocean. They were brought to Hawaii around 1940 in an attempt at a form of **biocontrol**. Jewel wasps are known to kill cockroaches, which are considered pests and have high populations in Hawaii.

TERRIFYING TRUTHS

Jewel wasps live mostly in tropical, or warm and wet, climates.

The jewel wasp was not a very successful form of biocontrol in Hawaii, because it usually only hunts in very small areas.

LET THE HUNT BEGIN

Jewel wasps have great senses of smell and sight, which they use to find cockroaches. In order to take down a much larger cockroach, the jewel wasp uses the element of surprise. It needs to strike quickly before the cockroach can get away!

The jewel wasp's first attack is to the cockroach's thorax. The wasp stings the cockroach between its first pair of legs. The cockroach becomes unable to move those legs and can't fight back.

TERRIFYING TRUTHS

After the cockroach is unable to move, it can't put up a fight and the jewel wasp gains control.

Cockroaches are sometimes more than six times larger than the jewel wasp!

BRAIN SURGERY

Human brain **surgeons** train for years. Jewel wasps are born with the skills they need. Their next sting is to the cockroach's brain.

The jewel wasp has special **sensors** on its stinger. The sensors help it find its way to the right spot. It lets out a poison, or venom, in two places in the brain. The venom makes the cockroach act like a zombie! The cockroach won't leave the spot where the wasp left it. It stays and cleans itself, waiting for the wasp's next direction.

TERRIFYING TRUTHS

As a zombie, the cockroach still has the ability to move. However, the jewel wasp seems to take away the cockroach's ability to make the choice to leave.

Even if the jewel wasp leaves,
the zombie cockroach stays put
and waits for its master to return.

13

PLANTING EGGS

The jewel wasp leaves the zombie cockroach to find a **burrow**. The wasp returns to the cockroach and drinks its blood. Then it bites down on the cockroach's antenna. It leads the cockroach by the antenna into its burrow, and the cockroach follows willingly.

The wasp lays one egg on the cockroach's body. It traps the cockroach in the burrow using small rocks. Then the wasp flies off to find other hosts for its many eggs.

TERRIFYING TRUTHS

Jewel wasps have multiple eggs to lay. However, they lay only one on each cockroach or fly.

The jewel wasp removes part of the cockroach's antennae and drinks its blood. The cockroach doesn't even try to fight back.

15

AN INSIDE JOB

In a couple of days, the egg breaks open. The baby wasp is called a larva. It chews through the cockroach's body and climbs inside. The larva eats the cockroach's **organs** one at a time. All this time, the zombie cockroach is still alive!

The larva grows stronger. It finally kills the cockroach, leaving only a shell. The larva "cleans" the cockroach shell. It stays there for about a month as it grows into adulthood. Then, the adult wasp breaks out of the cockroach's empty body.

TERRIFYING TRUTHS

The jewel wasp larva lets out a kind of matter on the empty cockroach's body that **sanitizes** it.

The jewel wasp comes out of the cockroach, already an adult and ready for the world.

17

JEWEL WASPS AND PEOPLE

Jewel wasps might live in cockroach nightmares, but they're usually not harmful to people. We are far too big for them to sting our brains! They're much more interested in going after victims they can plant their eggs in.

Jewel wasps are sometimes helpful to people. Cockroaches are unwanted insects and often treated as pests. Their populations also grow very quickly! Jewel wasps have no problem killing these pests and using them to raise their larvae.

TERRIFYING TRUTHS

Cockroaches can leave droppings and germs behind in homes. They can sometimes make people very sick.

Cockroaches are major pests in homes in warm climates.

19

A DEADLY STING

Are jewel wasps hardened killers or the world's best mothers? They attack cockroaches to keep their babies safe. It's good news for the larvae and very bad news for the cockroach.

Adult jewel wasps only live for a few months, but that's all the time they need. Female jewel wasps attack and lay eggs on dozens of cockroaches. Their system of killing is the stuff of horror movies and scary stories. These smart and skilled brain surgeons show that small, pretty bugs can be nightmare killers!

TERRIFYING TRUTHS

Other parasites can control their hosts, too. A certain parasitic fungus has been known to control ants and guide them to their death.

Sometimes the smallest parasites can do the most harm.

GLOSSARY

biocontrol: the reduction in the number of pests through changes to their surroundings

burrow: a hole made by an animal in which it lives or hides

climate: the average weather conditions of a place over a period of time

develop: to grow and change

fungus: a living thing that is somewhat like a plant, but doesn't make its own food, have leaves, or have a green color

host: the animal or plant on or in which a parasite lives

insect: a small, often winged, animal with six legs and three main body parts

organ: a part inside an animal's body

sanitize: to make clean

sensor: a tool or body part that can sense changes in its surroundings

surgeon: a doctor who conducts operations that include cutting into someone's body

victim: someone or something that is harmed by something else

FOR MORE INFORMATION

BOOKS

Johnson, Rebecca L. *Zombie Makers: True Stories of Nature's Undead*. Minneapolis, MN: Millbrook Press, 2013.

Rake, Matthew. *Creepy, Crawly Creatures*. Minneapolis, MN: Hungry Tomato, 2016.

WEBSITES

Cockroaches
pestworldforkids.org/pest-guide/cockroaches/
Learn more about the pesky insect jewel wasps control.

Emerald Cockroach Wasp Facts!
ipfactly.com/jewel-wasp/
Read more about this interesting wasp here.

Wasp
animals.nationalgeographic.com/animals/bugs/wasp/
This page has information on all different kinds of wasps.

INDEX

abdomen 6

adult 16, 17, 20

Africa 8

antennae 6, 14, 15

Asia 8

biocontrol 8, 9

brain 12, 18, 20

burrow 14

cockroach 4, 6, 8, 10, 11,
        12, 13, 14, 15, 16, 17,
        18, 19, 20

color 4, 6, 7

egg 14, 16, 18, 20

emerald cockroach wasp 4

Hawaii 8, 9

host 4, 14, 20

larvae 16, 18, 20

parasite 4, 20, 21

sting 10, 12, 18

stinger 6, 12

thorax 6, 10

venom 12

wings 6

zombie 12, 13, 14, 16